W9-BMY-926

ANCIENT CIVILIZATIONS AND THEIR MYTHS AND LEGENDS

NATIVE AMERICAN CIVILIZATIONS

Burlington, WA 98233

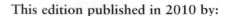

This edition published in 2010 by:

The Rosen Publishing Group, Inc.
29 East 21st Street
New York, NY 10010

Additional end matter copyright © 2010 by The Rosen Publishing Group, Inc.

Cover design by Nelson Sa.

Photo Credits: Cover, pp. 1, 3 © www.istockphoto.com/John Watson.

Library of Congress Cataloging-in-Publication Data

Mathis, Andy, 1969–
Native American civilizations / Andy Mathis and Marion Wood ; illustrations by Francesca D'Ottavi.
    p. cm.—(Ancient civilizations and their myths and legends)
Includes bibliographical references and index.
ISBN-13: 978-1-4042-8036-6 (library binding)
1. Indian mythology—North America. I. Wood, Marion, 1945– II. D'Ottavi, Francesca. III. Title.
E98.R3M337 2010
398.2089'97—dc22

2009011139

Manufactured in the United States of America

Copyright © McRae Books, Florence, Italy.

ANCIENT CIVILIZATIONS AND THEIR MYTHS AND LEGENDS

NATIVE
AMERICAN
CIVILIZATIONS

ANDY MATHIS
AND MARION WOOD

rosen publishing's
rosen
central
New York

CONTENTS

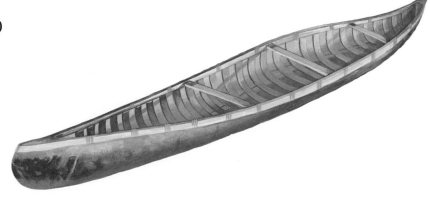

INTRODUCTION

Native Americans believed that supernatural power was all around them—not just in living things like animals and birds, but also in trees, mountains, and rivers, in the sun, moon, and stars, in thunder, wind, and rain. Myths helped to explain much of what people found puzzling or frightening. In an environment that was often harsh and unpredictable, they helped people to understand the forces that affected their lives, and why good or bad events happened. They described how the world began, why things came to be as they are, and how the balance of nature should be maintained.

Myths were also a way of reinforcing tribal customs and rules of behavior. This was important for people who lived in small, close-knit groups and had to work together in harmony. Breaking the rules could lead to disaster not only for the offender, but also for the whole community.

Because myths reflected people's lives and their experiences of the world around them, they varied from one area to another. Hunting tribes, for example, told many myths about animals, why they looked or behaved as they did, and how they ought to be treated when they were being hunted. Farming tribes, on the other hand, were more concerned with the supernatural beings that controlled rainfall and the growth of their crops. People still learn about their traditional myths through hearing them told or by seeing them acted out in dances and ceremonies.

HOW THIS BOOK WORKS

The book is divided into sections. Each one starts with a myth strikingly illustrated on a black background. This is followed by a nonfiction spread about one of the main Native American groups. The last spread is a myth telling of the coming of the Europeans to North America.

Spread with myth about buffalo leads on to a nonfiction one on the Native Americans of the Plains where the buffalo lived.

THE CREATION OF THE WORLD

In the beginning, people lived in the sky. The world below was covered by a vast expanse of water, and only fish and birds lived there.

One day one of the Sky People, a young woman, became ill. Her brothers, hearing that a powerful medicine was buried under an ancient apple tree, carried her there. They laid Sky Woman down beside the tree and began to dig.

For hours they worked, until there was a deep crater around the tree, but still no medicine was found. All at once, with a noise like thunder, the edges of the crater gave way. The brothers scrambled to safety, but to their horror both the tree and Sky Woman fell into the crater and vanished from sight.

Two swans gliding on the ocean below heard the distant rumble and looked up to see the tree and the woman tumbling from the sky. Hastily spreading their wings, they caught Sky Woman on their backs. A moment later, the apple tree crashed into the water beside them and sank into the depths. The swans turned their long necks and gazed at Sky Woman in astonishment.

"Who is it?" they whispered to one another. "Where has she come from? What shall we do with her?"

They sought the advice of the Big Turtle, oldest and wisest of all the creatures. Big Turtle stretched his neck from his shell and peered at Sky Woman, while the other animals and birds waited expectantly.

After much thought Big Turtle spoke, slowly and gravely: "The swans cannot carry their burden forever," he said. "We must make an island where she can live. We can build it from the earth clinging to the roots of the apple tree and I will support it on my back. Who will go and find some earth for me?"

Otter, Muskrat, and Beaver volunteered and, one by one, they dived down to look for the sunken tree. They were gone for a long time, but when they reappeared, tired and gasping, none of them had

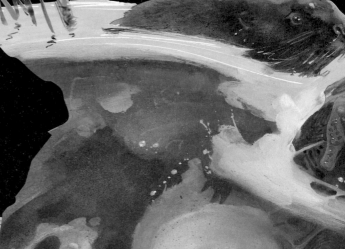

found a trace of it. It seemed as if Big Turtle's idea was doomed to failure.

Suddenly, another voice piped up. "Let me go! I'll find some earth for you!"

It was Toad and, before anyone could stop her, she had disappeared. The other creatures shook their heads in disbelief at her foolishness. How could small, insignificant Toad hope to succeed where the best swimmers had failed?

Toad was gone for a very long time and the waiting animals feared the worst. But, at long last, her head broke the surface and she spat a mouthful of earth onto Big Turtle's shell before sinking back exhausted.

All the creatures set to work spreading the earth over Big

Turtle's shell and, as they worked, the island grew until it was big enough for Sky Woman to step ashore. The island continued to grow until it became the world where we live today, which, some people say, is still carried on Big Turtle's back.

The Native Americans

8

America was discovered thousands of years ago by nomadic hunters who crossed from Asia in pursuit of animals like mammoth, mastodon, giant sloth, and others now long extinct. Over many centuries, small bands of hunters spread southward until they inhabited the whole continent from northernmost Alaska to the tip of South America. By the time Columbus arrived in 1492, there were millions of people living in North America alone, divided into some three hundred tribes and speaking more than two hundred separate languages.

During the Ice Age, the Bering Strait, the stretch of water that today separates the continents of Asia and North America, was dry land. This created a kind of "land bridge" over which the newcomers from Asia came, driven by the desire to hunt the animals they were following and perhaps also by natural curiosity.

Different regions, different lifestyles

The lives of the Native Americans varied according to where they lived. As with all people, finding food and shelter was their most important concern. On the Northwest Coast, for example, fish was plentiful and easily caught, so people lived mainly by fishing. In the Eastern Woodlands, the land was fertile, so most people were farmers. In such areas, where food was abundant, people had a settled way of life in villages of well-built houses. Inland, or where it was too cold or dry for farming—for example, in the Northern Forests or on the Plains—people lived by hunting. Because the game animals moved according to the season, the hunters had to move, too. Their homes were light, portable shelters, which were quick to put up and take down.

The arrival of the Europeans

Columbus had sailed westward from Spain seeking a new trade route to the East. When he landed in America in 1492, he believed that he had reached India and, because of his mistake, the native inhabitants became known as "Indians." Many of their present-day descendants now prefer to be known as Native Americans.

Climate, landscape, and cultural groups

North America is a huge continent with many types of landscape and climate. The Native Americans who lived there have been divided into seven cultural groups according to the type of environment they inhabited.

Wherever they lived, people usually understood their environment and made good use of it and, according to the natural resources available, developed skills such as woodworking, skin-dressing, basketry, and weaving.

1. The Northern Forests
South of the Arctic lies a cold, low-lying region of forests, rivers, lakes, and marshes, known as the Northern Forests.

2. The Northwest Coast
Toward the West, the land becomes more rugged and mountainous and, beyond the mountains, the rocky North Pacific coastline stretches from southern Alaska to northern California. Here, the climate is warmer and wetter, producing thick forests and undergrowth.

3. California
California is rich in resources, with wooded hills and river valleys inland and fertile grasslands along the coast.

4. The Plateau and Basin
Farther inland, between the Sierra Nevada and the Rocky Mountains, lies a vast wilderness of mountain and desert, known as the Plateau and Basin.

5. The Plains
On the other side of the Rockies, and stretching to the Mississippi River, lie the Plains, an area of rolling grasslands and prairies, where once herds of buffalo, several million strong, grazed.

6. The Southwest
To the southwest of the Plains, the land rises to form a great sandstone plateau, cut by the effects of wind and water into deep canyons and steep-sided mesas. Here, although the river valleys are wooded and well-watered, much of the rest of the land is dry and semidesert.

7. The Eastern Woodlands
Beyond the Mississippi, stretching from the semitropical swamplands of Florida northward along the Atlantic Seaboard to the St. Lawrence River, are the Eastern Woodlands, a fertile area of woods, lakes, and rivers.

RAVEN AND THE FIRST HUMAN BEINGS

The world was newly made. Raven flew over land and sea and admired what he had helped to create. He soared above forests and mountains where deer grazed among the trees and goats scrambled over the rocks. Gliding over streams and rivers, he saw beavers at work on their dams and glimpsed the silver flash of a leaping salmon. He swooped low over the ocean and saw that it teemed with fish and shellfish of every kind. Raven flew down and landed on a narrow strip of beach. He folded his wings and looked about him with satisfaction. The sun shone and the sea sparkled. Seals and sea lions basked on nearby rocks. Seabirds wheeled high overhead and in the distance, far out to sea, a whale spouted.

Suddenly, Raven's sharp eyes caught a slight movement by his feet. Bending down, he saw a stream of small bubbles escaping from something half-buried in the wet sand. It was a large clamshell and, as Raven watched, it began very slowly to open. From inside there came a faint sighing and murmuring, like a breeze ruffling the surface of the sea. To his amazement, Raven saw a little face craning forward, peering cautiously around. Then it caught sight of Raven and, with a startled gasp, shot back inside the shell, which snapped shut once more. Raven hopped around the clamshell and examined it from all sides. He prodded it with his beak. The shell remained tightly closed. Raven tapped it impatiently. "Come out!" he whispered, "Come out!" Very gradually, the shell opened a fraction and the little face peeped out again. This time it was followed by another little face, then another and another, until there were a whole row of faces, gazing at Raven half in fear and half in wonder. As the shell opened a little more, Raven saw that it was full of little people—the very first human beings!

With Raven nodding encouragement, they slowly uncurled themselves from the depths of the clamshell and stepped out onto the sand. They stretched their arms and legs in the warm sunshine and whispered excitedly to one another as they looked around at the strange new world in which they found themselves. Raven was elated by his discovery. He told the human beings that, because they had been born on the shore, they belonged to both the sea and the land. Before he flew away, he taught them

how to fish and how to work wood so that they could make their livelihood from the riches around them. The human beings increased in number and spread all along the Northwest coast, making their homes along the shore between the sea and the forest-clad mountains. Thanks to Raven's teaching, they became successful fishermen and skillful woodcarvers and grew wealthy and powerful as a result.

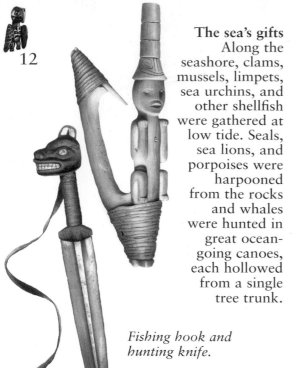

The sea's gifts
Along the seashore, clams, mussels, limpets, sea urchins, and other shellfish were gathered at low tide. Seals, sea lions, and porpoises were harpooned from the rocks and whales were hunted in great ocean-going canoes, each hollowed from a single tree trunk.

The Northwest Coast

The people who lived along the rocky North Pacific coastline obtained almost everything they needed either from the sea or from the forest. The sea provided them with food in abundance. Hooks, nets, spears, and traps were used to catch many kinds of fish—cod, halibut, sturgeon, herring, and the eulachon or candlefish, which was prized for its oil. When it had been dried, this fish would burn to give light like a candle. But it was the salmon that was the most important fish of all.

Fishing hook and hunting knife.

The forest's gifts
The dense forests of cedar, spruce, and fir also provided food—wild plants and berries, and game like deer, elk, and mountain goats. More importantly, however, the forests supplied the raw materials from which people built their houses and canoes, made baskets, mats, and clothing, and shaped containers, tools, and utensils of all kinds.

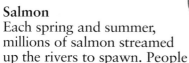

Decorated wooden model of a salmon used as a family crest.

Salmon
Each spring and summer, millions of salmon streamed up the rivers to spawn. People feasted richly on the fresh fish and dried or smoked the surplus to store for the coming winter.

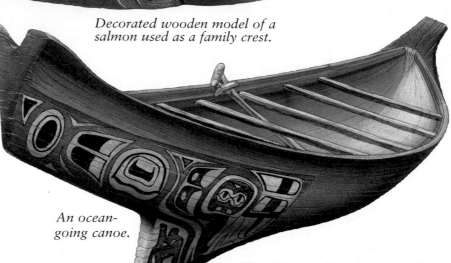

An ocean-going canoe.

The villages of large wooden houses were sited between the forests and the narrow beaches where canoes could be drawn up.

Masks

During special feasts and ceremonies, masked and costumed dancers re-enacted the exploits of the supernatural beings depicted on the crest poles. The dances were often highly dramatic, involving special effects and conjuring tricks.

Many masks, like this one, were hinged and could be operated with hidden strings so that beaks could clack open and shut, or whole masks burst apart to show other masks underneath. In a shadowy room lit only by the flames from a central fire, the carved and painted wooden masks brought mythical heroes, giants, and monsters terrifyingly to life.

Houses

Each house, built from large cedar planks split from the living tree, was often home to several families. The front of the house, facing the beach, was often elaborately painted or had a huge wooden house-post carved with the figures of animals, birds, and people built against it. House-posts were one type of crest or "totem" pole for which this part of North America is famous. Both the painting and the carving had a heraldic purpose, like a family crest or coat of arms, and represented legendary characters and events in the ancestral history of those who lived in the house.

Freestanding crest poles

Other types of crest pole were freestanding and commemorated important events or people. Many objects, even everyday ones like storage boxes, food bowls, spoons, tools and weapons, were also decorated with carved and painted crest designs.

Inside the houses, a wooden platform ran around the walls, where people worked, slept, and stored their belongings. Mats woven from soft cedar bark covered the platform and hung on the walls to stop drafts.

COYOTE AND WOLF

When the world first began, the only inhabitants were animals. These animals were not the ones familiar to us today. They were bigger, stronger, and smarter, and some of them looked different, too. Bear, for example, had a long tail until Coyote tricked him into dipping it in an icy stream and it was frozen off. Coyote himself once had beautiful blue fur, but his pride caused him to fall in the dust, and so coyotes have been dust-colored ever since.

Many of these animals behaved just as human beings do now. They wore clothes and lived in houses, they went hunting and fishing, and they fought with one another. They even looked like human beings sometimes, for they could change into any shape they had a mind to. When the real human beings came along later, animals changed into the ones we know now.

The two most important animals were Wolf and his younger brother, Coyote. Between them they helped to shape the world as it is today. Wolf did this because he wanted to make the world happy and pleasant, but Coyote, who was foolish and deceitful, usually did it by mistake or as a practical joke.

Unfortunately, Coyote's tricks often backfired, leaving him a sadder, though not always wiser, animal.

In the beginning, for example, Wolf had wanted death to be only temporary so that when people died, they could be brought back to life again. Coyote, just to be difficult, argued against this and so it was agreed that death should be final. When Coyote's own son died, he begged Wolf to change this rule, but Wolf refused, pointing out that it was Coyote who had insisted on it in the first place.

Sometimes Coyote's trickery brought good results. Crane had stolen all the fire in the world for himself so that the other animals had no means of cooking or keeping warm. Coyote disguised himself with a wig made from reeds and stole into Crane's camp at night while there was a dance going on. Joining in unnoticed, Coyote danced nearer and nearer the fire and, at the right moment, dipped his wig into the flames. The dry reeds caught alight instantly and Coyote dashed off into the night, carrying aloft his wig, now blazing like a torch. The other animals helped him to carry the fire all over the country so that now everyone can benefit from it.

Hunters in the Basin used decoys of ducks like this one to attract migrating birds. They floated them in the marshes and then waited for the wild birds to land.

The Plateau and Basin

The people who lived in the region known as the High Plateau had much in common with those who lived on the Northwest Coast and on the Plains to the east. Some tribes ventured across the Rocky Mountains to hunt buffalo on the Plains and to trade with the people who lived there, bartering dried fish, seashells, and corn husk bags for buffalo robes and meat. As a result of this contact with the Plains tribes, many of the Plateau people adopted their customs, wearing beaded buckskin, living in tepees, and becoming skilled and daring horse riders.

To the south of the Plateau lies the Great Basin, where both vegetation and wildlife are sparse. Early European explorers called it the "Great American Desert" and found it hard to imagine that anyone could survive in such a barren region. The tribes who lived there were among the poorest of all Native Americans, but they were skilled in making the best use of what the land had to offer.

Hunting

Men from the Basin hunted antelope and rabbits as well as birds, lizards, and even insects. Several families often banded together to hunt grasshoppers, driving the swarms toward a waiting fire where they were roasted before being made into soup or dried for storage.

Basket and beater used for gathering seeds.

Moccasins made by the Ute people in the Basin.

Finding food in the Basin

People foraged for anything that was edible. Women gathered all kinds of seeds, nuts, roots, and berries and made a great variety of special basket-work tools and containers to help them do so. Fan-shaped beaters, for example, were used to dislodge seeds and berries into flat trays, which were then emptied into large conical baskets for carrying back to the camp. Pine nuts, in particular, were a favorite food and special ceremonies were held to welcome the pine nut harvest in late summer and early autumn.

Life in the "Great American Desert"

When the weather was warm, people wore little or no clothing, coating their bare skin with mud to protect themselves from mosquitoes and other troublesome insects. Their homes were simple brush shelters, easily built as needed and abandoned when they moved on. In winter they camped in sheltered canyons or caves, keeping warm with rabbitskin cloaks.

Colorful
decoration for
the horse's
forehead

Beaded
collar

Decorative
saddlecloth

Hunting

Deer, antelope, and bighorn sheep were hunted in the mountains. The horns of mountain sheep were used to make bowls and spoons and horn bows, which were more powerful than wooden bows and fired arrows with greater range and accuracy.

Storage bag made of hemp and corn husk.

Some groups of Plateau peoples, like the Nez Percé, became noted breeders and traders of horses, building up herds several hundred strong. The distinctive spotted horse known as the Appaloosa was particularly highly valued.

This decorated bowl was carved from the horn of a bighorn sheep. Precious objects of this kind were used as items of exchange in many areas of the Plateau.

Fishing

Like their northern neighbors, the people of the Plateau were skillful fishermen. Most villages held fishing rights along the streams and rivers, where great quantities of salmon were caught. In some areas fishermen built special wooden platforms projecting out over weirs constructed in the rivers, where they could trap and spear the salmon. As well as being eaten fresh, salmon was smoked and dried so that it could be stored for use in winter when other food was scarce.

THE ACORN HATS

According to some Californian tribes, the first people to inhabit the world were the Ikxareyavs. They prepared the way for human beings and became the animals, birds, and plants that exist today.

For several days, wisps of smoke had been seen on the distant mountains. The Ikxareyavs knew that this heralded the appearance of human beings. Everyone rushed to prepare for the new arrivals.

The Acorn Girls were hard at work weaving new caps for the occasion. The two elder sisters, Maul Oak Girl and Black Oak Girl, were both skillful weavers. They deftly twisted and knotted hazel shoots, pine roots, grass, and fern stems into intricate patterns of gold and brown and black. Tan Oak Girl, the youngest sister, was not such a good weaver. She was slow and clumsy and try as she might, the twigs and shoots would not bend as pliantly or lie as smoothly as her awkward fingers wished. She was aware of her sisters' scorn, and her cheeks reddened as she overheard their mocking whispers and laughter.

Almost together, with whoops of triumph, Maul Oak Girl and Black Oak Girl bounded to their feet, their finished caps on their heads. The caps were very beautiful, well-shaped, and finely woven, and the two girls turned this way and that, admiring each other.

"Now we are ready to go!" declared Maul Oak Girl. "We must hurry if we are to get to the woods in time."

"Please don't go without me!" cried Tan Oak Girl. "Please wait! Look—I've almost finished!" And she turned her cap inside out to trim off the loose ends.

"We can't wait," the others called. "If you aren't ready, we must leave you behind."

Tan Oak Girl hastily crammed on her cap, still inside out, and ran after them. When her sisters saw her cap, with untrimmed spikes of grass and twigs sticking out all over it, they burst out laughing. "What a sight you are!" they cried. "The

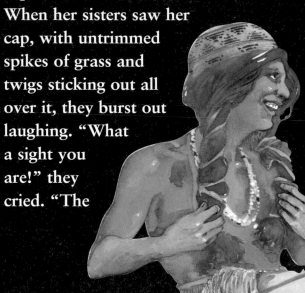

human beings won't want anything to do with you!" Suddenly they stopped, for the human beings had just arrived and had heard their cruel words.

The human beings spoke kindly to Tan Oak Girl. "Although your cap is not as pretty as the others," they said, "you will provide the best food and because of you, people will never go hungry."

Shy and embarrassed, Tan Oak Girl hid her face inside her cap.

Her sisters, overcome with shame, did the same. They grew smaller and smaller until they turned into the acorns we know today. Tan Oak acorns still have rough and prickly caps, but they taste the best and people prefer them to acorns like those of Maul Oak and Black Oak, which are harder to pound into flour and not as good to eat.

California

The Native Californians lived in a land full of natural resources. Food was both varied and abundant. Inland, the hills and woods were full of deer, rabbits, squirrels, and birds, while the lakes and rivers teemed with fish and waterfowl. Those living along the Pacific coast lived well on the plentiful fish and shellfish available to them. The rich vegetation also provided the raw materials for many purposes. In northern California people lived in houses built of wooden planks, rather like those of the Northwest coast. Elsewhere, houses were usually dome-shaped huts made of wooden poles covered with reeds or sheets of bark. Reeds were also used for weaving mats and mattresses, and bundles of reeds tied together made rafts for crossing lakes and rivers.

Tan oak

Black oak

Maul oak

The acorn harvest
As well as hunting and fishing, people gathered many different kinds of plants, seeds, nuts, and berries for food. The acorn harvest was very important. Because acorns contain tannic acid, they can be unpleasant, or even poisonous, to eat. So they must be specially treated to make them edible. The shelled acorns were ground into flour or meal, and then water was poured through the meal to rinse out the bitter-tasting acid. Acorn meal was very nourishing and people ate it as porridge or soup, or baked into bread or cakes.

A Wintu woman's skirt made of pine nut shells and buckskin.

Warm cloak made from twisted strips of rabbits' fur sewn together.

Clothing
Plant materials were also used for making items of clothing, although, because of the warm climate, not many clothes were worn. Women wore skirts of plant fiber or shredded bark and round basketwork caps. In cold weather, people wrapped up in deerskin cloaks or blankets woven from strips of rabbit skin.

Basketry

Californian women were renowned as basket makers. They wove their baskets from the materials available all around them—pine roots and shoots of willow and hazel, black maidenhair fern stems, and shiny yellow bear grass. Baskets were used for gathering and storing food, and some were so tightly woven that they could be used for carrying water and even for cooking. Food placed in a basket was cooked by dropping into it stones that had been heated in a fire. The stones had to be stirred frequently to prevent them from burning holes in the bottom of the cooking basket.

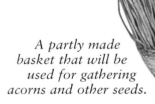

Native Californian women wore basketwork hats. They used a mixture of tree roots, shoots, grass, and fern stems to create interesting designs.

Large baskets like this one were used for gathering and carrying seeds.

A partly made basket that will be used for gathering acorns and other seeds.

Measuring wealth

Wealth was often measured in terms of items such as deerskins, feathers, obsidian knives, and shells. Strings of valuable dentalium or tooth shells were used as a form of money and stored in purses carved from elk antler.

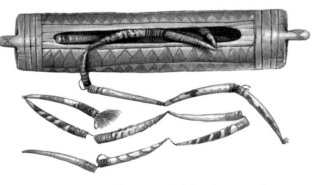

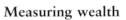

Ceremonial baskets and costumes

As well as everyday baskets, there were special baskets intended as gifts or for use in ceremonies. These baskets were particularly finely woven and richly decorated. Often they were entirely covered with colorful feathers of brilliant scarlet and yellow and iridescent green and hung with beads and pendants cut from clamshell and abalone. Elaborate feather headdresses and costumes, trimmed with shell beads and pendants, were made for ceremonies and dances. Such items were very expensive and were regarded as proof of the owner's wealth.

This beautifully decorated gift basket was made by a Pomo woman from northern California.

THE BOY WHO WAS KEPT BY A BEAR

A boy, lost in the forest, was found by a bear, who took pity on him and adopted him as his own son. He cared for the boy throughout the summer, teaching him to hunt and fish and showing him where

the bees kept their honey and where the best berries grew. When autumn came, he took the boy up into the mountains to his winter den. It was warm and dry, and the bear kept it well stocked with food.

The boy's father had never lost hope of finding his son. He looked for him each time he went hunting and it so happened that, as the first snows of winter began to fall, his footsteps took him toward the bear's den. Although he was still far distant, the bear sensed his approach and resolved to use all his powers to distract him from his quest.

Taking a porcupine carcass from his larder, he threw it out of the den. At that very moment, many miles away, the hunter noticed where a porcupine had gnawed a tree by the forest track. He thought of pursuing the animal, but decided instead to leave it for the time being and continued on his way.

The bear next threw out a beaver carcass, just as the distant hunter was passing a lake. The man noticed that some beavers had built a lodge there and made a note to set a trap on his way back. Finally the bear threw out a partridge and at that very instant a partridge whirred across the

hunter's path. Again he was tempted to follow the bird, but again he decided to return for it later.

As a last resort the bear conjured up a fierce storm of howling wind and whirling snow, but still the boy's father struggled on, every step bringing him closer and closer to the bear's den.

The bear groaned in despair, "I cannot defeat him! He is walking straight to me!" The boy tried to comfort him, but the bear said, "Do not be sad. I know that I am soon to die, but I can still help you to become a mighty hunter. When I am dead, cut off one of my forelegs and wrap it up in soft buckskin. Keep this bundle hanging up in your tent above the place where you always sit. When you want to hunt bear, find a spot from where you can survey the whole countryside and look for a place where smoke is rising. Only you will be able see this and there you will always find a bear."

At that moment the boy's father broke through the snow covering the entrance to the bear's den. The bear went to meet him and was killed. The boy returned home with his father, but he never forgot the bear. He kept his friend's foreleg just as he had been told and grew up to be a very successful hunter.

The Northern Forests

Forests of spruce, pine, cedar, and larch span the North American continent from the Labrador coast to Alaska. Here, the bitterly cold winter lasts many months, with freezing winds and snow and few daylight hours. The summer is warm but very short and plagued by swarms of biting insects. Life for the Native Americans in these northern forests was often hard and unpredictable. The search for food was all-important and never-ending. There was often starvation and death, especially during the long winter.

The painted skull of a bear and its forelegs, wrapped in bark or skin, were often tied to a tree near a hunting camp as a mark of respect.

Hunting

People lived by hunting and fishing, and later, as the European fur trade became more important, by trapping animals like beaver, muskrat, and squirrel for their skins. Hunters and their families were constantly on the move, following the animals on which they depended for their livelihood.

Fur-lined hood

Fur-lined robe

Mittens

Wooden sled

Snowshoes

Most homes were portable wooden frameworks covered with skins or bark. Only in the west of the region did the Ingalik people build more permanent winter houses of wood and turf.

Naskapi hunters wore caribou-skin coats painted with special designs intended to bring them success.

Clothing

Skins were very important for making clothing. Both men and women wore a shirt or parka, trousers or leggings, and moccasins. In cold weather they added mittens, a cap or hood, and a fur-lined robe. Dressing skins and making them into garments was a constant occupation for hunters' wives. A complete set of warm winter clothing might use as many as ten or eleven caribou skins, and a hunter needed a new set of clothing at least once a year.

Leggings

Moccasins

Animal skins had many uses. They were needed to make tent covers, arrow quivers, guncases, and bags and when cut into strips, ropes and fastenings of all kinds.

Moose and caribou

Moose and caribou, hunted for both meat and skins, were the most important game animals. The caribou herds were hunted in summer on open ground and in winter in the forests, where both people and animals could find shelter from the biting wind and snow. Snowshoes, made of wooden frames laced with rawhide strips, helped hunters to keep moving even where snow was deep.

Hunting customs

Hunting was bound up with rules intended to ensure that game remained plentiful. The bones of water creatures, like beaver and muskrat, were carefully returned to the lake or river with the words "Be made again in water." Bears were of great ceremonial importance and elaborate rituals surrounded their hunting and killing.

Snowshoes had wooden frames with woven rawhide webbing inside. Some snowshoes were long and narrow, while others were more rounded in shape, like the Naskapi ones shown here.

Basketry

The women of the Northern forests made waterproof baskets from birch and fir bark for cooking and keeping food. They also made many other baskets for storing and carrying their possessions. The shape of the baskets and the way they were decorated varied from region to region.

THE BUFFALO DANCE

For many weeks, no buffalo had been sighted on the Plains and people were starving. Early one morning, a girl went to fetch water from the river. To her surprise, she saw a herd of buffalo grazing peacefully on a nearby bluff, almost directly above a corral.

"Oh, buffalo!" she cried joyfully. "If you will only jump into the corral, I will marry one of you!"

She turned to alert the camp's hunters, but before she could move she heard the thundering of hoofs and saw the whole herd plunge over the edge of the bluff into the corral below. One great bull escaped and bounded toward her. She tried to escape, but the buffalo seized her and tossed her on his back.

"You promised to marry one of us if we jumped," he reminded her. "Now you will be my wife."

In vain the girl protested that she had only been joking. Unheeding, the buffalo carried her away over the prairie.

Her father set out to look for her and, after many miles came to a muddy waterhole. A herd of buffalo was grazing a little way off. To his delight, he saw his daughter coming toward him.

"I cannot return home with you," said the girl. "I have been sent for water and if I run away, the buffalo will follow and kill us both."

No sooner had she spoken than the buffalo herd was upon them. Snorting in fury, they trampled the man into the mud with their cruel hoofs so that not a trace of him remained.

"You see now how it is for us," said the buffalo. "So many of us have been killed by your people for food. But we will give you a chance. If you can restore your father to life, you may both return home."

As the girl sat weeping by the water hole, a magpie flew down beside her.

"Oh, please help me!" begged the girl. "Help me find my father's body."

The magpie jabbed the mud around the waterhole with his beak, and at last he pulled out a tiny piece of bone. The girl laid the bone on the ground and covered it with her buffalo robe. She began to sing and pray and such was the power of her songs and prayers that her father returned to life. When she lifted the robe, he stood up unharmed.

The buffalo were amazed. "You have strong powers," they said. "Now we will teach you our dance and song. You must never forget them."

When the girl and her father returned
home, they taught their people the
buffalos' song and their slow, stately
dance. This was how the warrior society
called the Buffalo Bulls came into
being and why they dance wearing
the skins and heads of the buffalo.

The Plains

The lives of the Plains tribes centered on the buffalo herds. Several families, including women and children, often joined together to hunt buffalo by driving them over a cliff or into a specially built corral. This was an enclosure made from wooden poles set upright in the ground to a height of several feet. From the entrance of the corral a fence extended outward to form a V-shaped trap. The mouth of the V was very wide, so hunters could drive or lure the buffalo inside without the animals suspecting that it was a trap. Once the buffalo were inside, the hunters pursued them more closely, while, at the same time, other members of the band leapt out from behind the fence, shouting and waving. This made the animals panic and rush into the corral, where they were killed with bows and arrows. Several hundred buffalo at a time could be killed in this way.

Plains war bonnet.

Headdress made from buffalo skin and horns.

Uses of the buffalo
As well as meat, the buffalo provided skins for clothing, saddlebags, and storage trunks, bones for tools, sinews for thread and bow strings, and horns for cups and spoons.

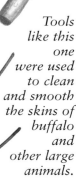

Tools like this one were used to clean and smooth the skins of buffalo and other large animals.

Tepees
The Plains tepee consisted of several buffalo skins sewn together and stretched over a number of poles. Easily put up and taken down, the tepee was an ideal home for these nomadic people. When horses were introduced, horse-drawn travois were used, which could carry greater quantities of food and equipment. Tepees became larger, since their owners could now transport longer poles and larger, heavier covers.

Tanned buffalo skin could be decorated with brightly colored patterns and designs and made into striking robes like the one this Plains woman is wearing.

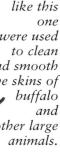

Warrior societies

Young men who wanted to join the warrior societies had first to prove themselves in battle by carrying out brave and daring exploits, such as stealing an enemy's horses or weapons, or touching him without being touched in return. It was also the way for a man to win the respect and admiration of his whole tribe. Warriors boasted of their exploits by reciting them at public gatherings and painted them on their buffalo robes, shirts, shields, and tepees. They often wore feathers or animal skins to show they had performed particular deeds. Some wore an eagle's feather for each enemy killed or trimmed their shirts with ermine skins to show that they had stolen guns from an enemy's camp.

Rattle used by the Buffalo Bulls Society during the Buffalo Calling Dance.

Horses

Horses, brought to America by Spanish explorers, reached the Plains in the 18th century and brought many changes. Once they had horses, the Plains' people were able to travel farther and faster than before. Hunters on horseback could chase and surround the buffalo herds.

Shield like the ones used by the Buffalo Bulls Society during ceremonial dancing.

Protecting the camp and keeping order were the duties of the warrior societies, clubs to which most of the men belonged. Within each tribe, there were several warrior societies, with names like Stone Hammers, Kit-foxes, and Buffalo Bulls. Each society had its own special songs, dances, and costumes.

Arapaho ceremonial axe with a wooden handle and a metal blade.

Summer meetings

For much of the year, people lived in small hunting groups scattered over the Plains, but in summer the whole tribe came together to form a great circle of tepees. For everyone it was an important and exciting time, an occasion for meeting, ceremonies, feasts, dances, and games.

THE SEARCH FOR THE CORN SISTERS

In the beginning the first people had only grass seeds to eat and, because they were always hungry, they begged the Seed People to send them something more. The Seed People took pity on them and sent them the six beautiful Corn Sisters.

In their blankets of purest white, edged with all the colors of the rainbow, the Corn Sisters moved gracefully through the grass and, as they moved, the plants grew tall and strong, bearing long leaves and silken tassels. The Corn Sisters gently peeled back the leaves and the people saw for the first time the six colors of corn—yellow, blue, red, white, speckled, and black.

For many years the Corn Sisters lived among the first people and were loved and honored by them for their goodness and kindness. In time, however, because the corn was so plentiful, the people became wasteful. They allowed weeds to choke their fields. They tore the ripe cobs roughly from the plants and shelled the corn carelessly so that much of it was trampled underfoot. They ground more cornmeal than they needed and threw away what they did not use. They no longer showed the Corn Sisters respect.

At last the Corn Sisters could endure no more. Drawing their blankets over their heads, they left the village and fled to the home of the Kachinas high in the mountains. The Kachinas, angered by their story, hid them at the bottom of a lake where the people would not be able to find them.

At first, the people paid little heed. They continued to squander their corn so that when planting time came, very little seed corn remained. They sowed what they had, but the plants were sickly and the few ears harvested were pale and shrivelled. The following harvest was worse and the next failed entirely.

Now the people were starving. They wanted to ask the Corn Sisters to forgive them and return, but they did not know where they had gone. They sent out messengers, but no one could find them. At last they begged the help of Paiyatuma, the flute-player, who, since the world began, had brought the dew and mists of dawn to freshen the earth and the growing plants.

Realizing that the people had learned a bitter lesson, Paiyatuma agreed to their desperate pleas. He began to play and, as his music soared, it drew the Corn Sisters from the lake. The people

welcomed them back joyfully, and all that day, as Paiyatuma played his flute, the Corn Sisters danced once more in the fields.

The Corn Sisters did not remain among the people, but before they left forever, they gave them baskets of seed corn, one of each color—yellow, blue, red, white, speckled, and black. And the Kachinas taught the people the songs and ceremonies to honor the Corn Sisters, which Kachina dancers still perform today.

The Southwest—The Farmers

The Pueblo people of the Southwest take their name from the Spanish word for a village—"pueblo"—the name given to them by the first Europeans to explore the region at the end of the 16th century. The Spanish explorers were greatly impressed by the way of life they found there, and especially by the large villages—or pueblos—built of stone and adobe. Some of the pueblos were already centuries old when the Spanish explorers arrived, and some are still occupied today. The Acoma pueblo in New Mexico, for example, is said to have been occupied continuously for more than a thousand years. The Pueblo people are not a single tribe. Each pueblo is independent, ruled by an elected governor and council, and several languages are spoken.

Pueblo children are given wooden dolls representing Kachinas so that they can learn about them and understand the stories behind the performances.

Rituals and dance

Because farming is difficult in this semi-desert region, the Pueblo people have developed a long and complicated series of ceremonies and dances designed to encourage rainfall, produce fruitful harvests, and generally bring good fortune to the pueblo.

This man is taking part in the Corn Dance. He has painted his body in black and white and carries a spruce branch in one hand and a rattle in the other.

Pueblo traditions continue to the present-day. This Hopi Kachina doll dates from 1930.

Ceremonies

Ceremonies play such an important part in Pueblo life that it has been estimated that some Pueblo men spend more than half their time taking part. Many ceremonies take the form of dramatic performances where masked dancers impersonate supernatural beings called Kachinas.

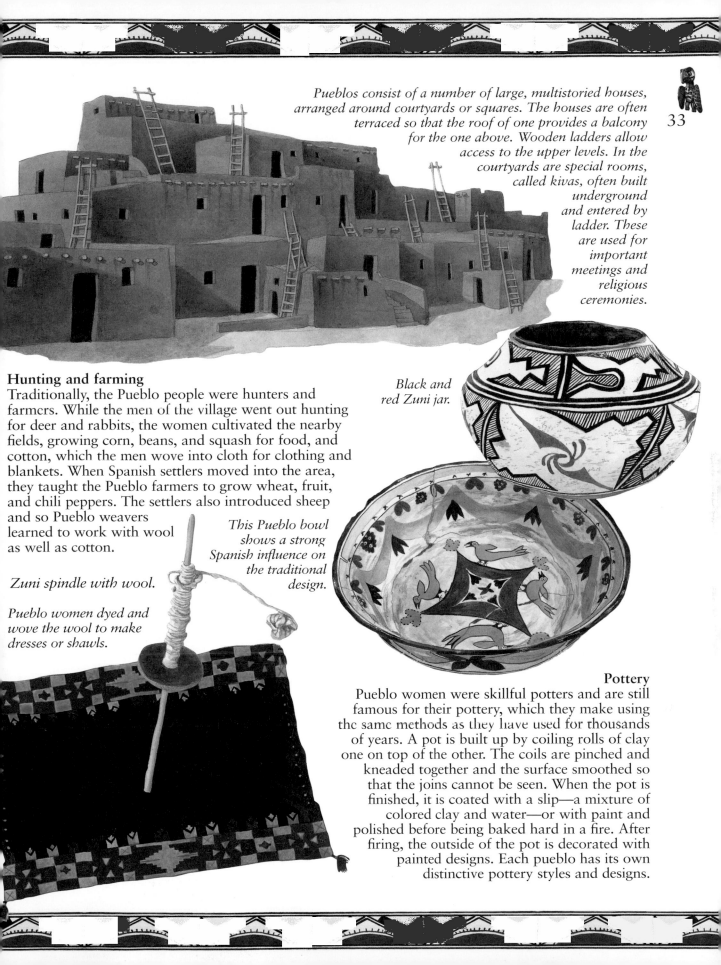

Pueblos consist of a number of large, multistoried houses, arranged around courtyards or squares. The houses are often terraced so that the roof of one provides a balcony for the one above. Wooden ladders allow access to the upper levels. In the courtyards are special rooms, called kivas, often built underground and entered by ladder. These are used for important meetings and religious ceremonies.

Hunting and farming

Traditionally, the Pueblo people were hunters and farmers. While the men of the village went out hunting for deer and rabbits, the women cultivated the nearby fields, growing corn, beans, and squash for food, and cotton, which the men wove into cloth for clothing and blankets. When Spanish settlers moved into the area, they taught the Pueblo farmers to grow wheat, fruit, and chili peppers. The settlers also introduced sheep and so Pueblo weavers learned to work with wool as well as cotton.

Black and red Zuni jar.

This Pueblo bowl shows a strong Spanish influence on the traditional design.

Zuni spindle with wool.

Pueblo women dyed and wove the wool to make dresses or shawls.

Pottery

Pueblo women were skillful potters and are still famous for their pottery, which they make using the same methods as they have used for thousands of years. A pot is built up by coiling rolls of clay one on top of the other. The coils are pinched and kneaded together and the surface smoothed so that the joins cannot be seen. When the pot is finished, it is coated with a slip—a mixture of colored clay and water—or with paint and polished before being baked hard in a fire. After firing, the outside of the pot is decorated with painted designs. Each pueblo has its own distinctive pottery styles and designs.

THE RAIN CHANT

A hunter, who had stopped by a river to rest from the midday sun, was surprised to see a baby girl swimming in the water. He returned at the same time for several days and again found the baby swimming there. One day, going earlier than usual, he hid in the reeds by the water's edge. As he watched, the baby rose to the surface and floated toward the bank. The hunter snatched her up and ran away as fast as he could. He stopped for a moment to look back and saw the river raging like a whirlpool. He ran on, not stopping until he got home.

The hunter and his wife adopted the child as their own daughter. When she was older, they told her how she had been found and the girl decided to visit the place. As she approached the river, she heard someone chopping wood. When she reached the bank, however, the sound stopped and there was no one there. She returned to the river the next day, and again the following day, and each time the same thing happened.

On the fourth day, her foster father said to her sadly, "I realize now that I stole you from the Holy People who live in the river. These offerings will ease your journey back to your old home."

He gave her a basket filled with precious stones and shells, sprinkled with pollen and river crystals, and once more the girl returned to the river. This time, a young man was standing on the bank. He frowned when he saw the girl.

"Why are you here?" he demanded. "This is the home of the Water Buffalo and no place for Earth Surface People."

The girl told her story and the young man nodded. "You must be the Water Buffalo baby who disappeared long ago," he said. "Follow me." And, rolling back the river like a blanket, he led her to the home of the Water Buffalo.

The Water Buffalo was large and imposing, with the horns and hoofs of a buffalo and the mane and tail of a horse. He welcomed the girl and accepted her basket of offerings graciously.

"I am glad that you have come," said the Water Buffalo. "I have something to give you before you return to the Earth Surface forever." And he gave her a little buckskin bag tied with a thong. "Your people must use this when they want rain. It contains the four winds and four mists, together with hair cut from my mane and mud from the river."

Then the Water Buffalo taught the girl the songs and prayers needed to bring rain, and showed her how to build the special hogan for the

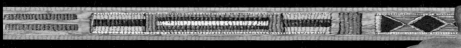

rain ceremony and
how to decorate it
with plants and flowers.

When the girl returned home,
she remembered everything
the Water Buffalo had
told her. She and her
descendants became
known as the
Meeting of the
Rivers People,
who knew how
to bring rain.

The Southwest—The Nomads

As well as being the home of the peaceful Pueblo farmers, the Southwest was also the territory of nomadic hunters and gatherers who arrived from the north sometime during the 15th century. These were the fierce, warlike Apaches, who swooped down from their mountain strongholds to raid the pueblos and the Spanish settlements, stealing their crops and driving off livestock. The herds of horses that they acquired in this way enabled them to range far and wide over the Southwest. Some Apache bands raided as far south as Mexico, while others crossed the Rio Grande into the southern Plains.

Domed brush wickiup shelters were roofed with thatch or bark.

Houses

Always on the move to escape retaliation, the Apaches lived in small, scattered family settlements. Those who lived in the wooded mountains and river valleys built wickiups. Other groups, like the Mescalero or Jicarillo, who had made contact with the Plains tribes, lived in skin tepees.

Burden baskets were used by Apache women to carry belongings during their frequent moves.

Lifestyles

Raiding was only one part of Apache life, although it was the part that struck fear into their neighbors. Less dramatically, they also hunted deer and antelope and collected wild plants, roots, and nuts for food. Like most gatherers, Apache women were skilled basketmakers and made a variety of beautifully decorated baskets and basketwork tools for collecting, transporting, and storing food.

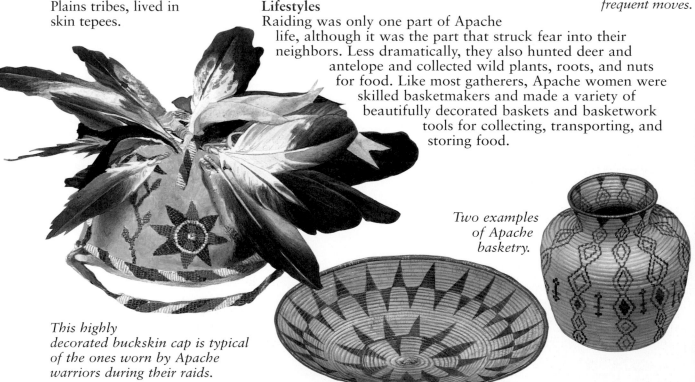

Two examples of Apache basketry.

This highly decorated buckskin cap is typical of the ones worn by Apache warriors during their raids.

From the local Spanish settlers the Navajo also learned to work silver and became famous for their silver jewelry, often set with semi-precious stones, particularly turquoise.

The Navajo
One Apache group became known as the Navajo. They settled among the Pueblos and learned many of their ways. Traditional Navajo houses are called hogans. Not many Navajo people live in hogans today, but they are still used for ceremonies, such as those held to cure sickness and to bring well-being and prosperity.

Hogans are circular or octagonal in shape and built of wooden poles or logs, covered with earth.

Navajo sandpainting ceremonies
Navajo ceremonies often include the making of sandpaintings. These illustrate scenes from Navajo myths and depict the Holy People, the supernatural beings who play important roles in the myths. The sandpainter, who combines the duties of priest and doctor, trickles finely ground colors made from sand, charcoal, cornmeal, pollen, and crushed flower petals between finger and thumb to make the sandpainting. When it is finished, the patient for whom the ceremony is being held sits on it and absorbs its power by having colors from various parts of the design applied to his or her body.

A sandpainting ceremony may take place over several days, with a number of different sandpaintings being made. As many as six hundred sandpainting designs have been recorded.

Classic Navajo blanket woven in the mid-19th century.

Pueblo influence
Although the Navajo did not give up hunting and remained nomadic for part of the year, they also became farmers, growing corn, vegetables, and fruit, and raising sheep. From the Pueblo they learned to weave, using the wool from their sheep to make brightly patterned blankets for their own use and for trade to other tribes and, later on, for sale to white settlers and tourists.

THE PLEIADES

There were once seven boys who spent all their time playing chunkey and gambling (see p. 40). Every morning they gathered at the chunk yard, an area of level sand near the townhouse. As soon as the chunkey stone was rolled along the ground, two of the boys hurled their poles after it, each attempting to hit it or prevent the other from doing so. Their friends cheered from the sidelines, counting up the scores and making bets on the outcome of the match. All day long the boys played this game, stopping only when darkness fell.

In vain their mothers reminded them of the work to be done in the fields—the planting, hoeing, and weeding, and all the labor of harvest. They pleaded, shouted, and scolded, but to no avail. There was nothing that could drag those boys away from the chunkey game. Finally, their mothers lost patience with them and decided to teach them a lesson.

That evening the boys returned home as usual for supper. Mouthwatering aromas filled the air and they took their places eagerly, expecting to find their bowls filled with delicious corn stew. Instead, the bowls contained nothing but chunkey stones. Mystified, they looked around. Everyone was laughing at them.

"What do you expect?" asked their mothers, smiling grimly. "Since you would rather play at chunkey than help us, you can feast on chunkey stones!"

Angry and resentful at the trick played on them, the boys rushed back to the chunk yard. They decided that they would leave home. They danced around the town house, slowly at first, then with gathering speed. Round and round they whirled, faster and faster, until their feet left the ground. As they rose into the air, their mothers tried to catch them, but the boys were beyond their reach. One of the mothers managed to pull her son down by hooking a chunkey pole into his belt, but he landed with such force that he sank into the ground and the earth closed over him.

The other boys soared higher until they were no more than pinpoints of light in the night sky. They became the cluster of stars known as the Pleiades and they are there in the heavens still.

The mother of the boy who sank into the earth visited the spot each day, watering it with her tears. A little green shoot appeared and grew into a tall pine tree. People said that it was the seventh boy, trying to rejoin his lost companions. The pine tree has never been able to reach the Pleiades, but its wood burns brightly and gives off sparks like shooting stars.

The Eastern Woodlands

The Eastern Woodlands stretch along the Atlantic Seaboard of North America from the Great Lakes to the Gulf of Mexico. The tribes who lived in this area were mainly farmers, cultivating their crops in fields laid out around their villages. All the clearing of the land, the digging, and the planting were done by hand, using stone axes and sticks and hoes with blades made from wood or shell or the shoulder blades of large animals. The earth was drawn up into mounds and five or six corn seeds were pushed into each, and later a few beans, and then a few squash seeds. The growing corn supported the climbing beans, while the trailing squash below helped to keep down the weeds.

After contact with the Europeans, a Cherokee man called Sequoyah invented a writing system. It consisted of 86 characters, one for each of the syllables of the Cherokee tongue.

Lacrosse

Lacrosse or stickball was played over the whole Woodlands area. It was an energetic and often dangerous game, played on a large open field by two opposing teams, with sometimes as many as a hundred players a side. Each team tried to pass a small ball toward the opposing goal using only their rackets to carry and throw the ball. Northeastern players used one racket to pass the ball while those in the Southeast used two.

Games

Games of skill or chance were popular and could last for many hours, with both players and spectators wagering their possessions on the results. One of the most popular Southeastern games was chunkey. This was a game for two players played on a special court or chunk yard.

The chunkey stone, a smooth stone disc, was sent rolling along the ground and each player tried to hit it by throwing a long wooden pole. Points were scored according to where and how the poles landed.

The arrival of European settlers

It was the people of the Eastern Woodlands who greeted the first European settlers, helping them to survive in their new homes and teaching them how to grow corn, build birchbark canoes, and smoke tobacco. Several Southeastern tribes adopted European ways, building churches and schools and developing a written alphabet. Alas, peaceful coexistence was rare and did not last. Of the tribes that once farmed this rich, fertile land, many have vanished forever.

Houses

Houses solidly built of wood, bark, and thatch were grouped in villages or towns, sometimes protected with a wooden stockade. There was usually a central square with a town house for meetings and ceremonies and, nearby, an area for games.

Houses in the hot southern regions consisted of a thatched roof and no walls, like this Seminole house in Florida.

41

Pestle for pounding corn.

Food

The Iroquois called the three main crops—corn, squash, and beans—the "Three Sisters." They were always planted and eaten together. Corn was the most important of the three. Roasted and ground into coarse flour, it was eaten at almost every meal in the form of bread or cakes or as porridge mixed with vegetables. In addition, people caught fish in the lakes and rivers and hunted deer and other animals with bows and arrows or with traps and snares. In the woods they also found a plentiful supply of wild plants, roots, nuts, and berries. In the Northeastern Woodlands, maple sap was collected in springtime and made into sugar and syrup to sweeten food.

Reconstruction of the prehistoric Cherokee capital, called Echota, which was situated on the Tennessee River.

Food was cooked over a fire, often using a system of four logs. As the logs burned they were pushed farther into the center where the fire was hottest and cooking was done.

THE FLOATING ISLAND

When the Algonkian hero Glooskap first arrived, the world was not as it is today. Animals were larger and stronger than they are now. The moose, tall as a mountain, trampled everything in its path. The squirrel tore down trees with its teeth, destroying whole forests in a single day. Knowing that the world could not survive if this persisted, Glooskap shrank the animals to their present sizes.

For a time all went well until one day the river, which served the whole country with pure clear water, ran dry. A greedy water monster had swallowed it all up. The monster was so huge that its body filled the whole river valley. Its mouth was a mile wide, its eyes stuck out like pine knots, and its bloated body was covered with huge warts. When Glooskap went to demand the water back, the monster opened its gaping mouth to swallow him up. But Glooskap made himself taller than the tallest pine tree and seized the monster in his huge hand. He squeezed until he had wrung every drop of water from it so that the river ran freely again.

Glooskap stayed to help and protect the world for thousands of years and during that time only one person managed to defeat him. While on a journey, Glooskap stopped to rest at a tepee. On the floor of the tepee sat a baby, smiling and crowing. Glooskap had never seen such a creature before and he ordered the baby to come to him. The baby laughed, but did not move. Glooskap frowned and then shouted at the baby, but it only began to howl loudly and Glooskap rushed from the tepee in despair. When babies today say "Goo-goo!", they are remembering how one of their number defeated the mighty Glooskap long, long ago.

One day, seabirds brought Glooskap news of a mysterious island drifting toward the shore. The excited birds told him that there were three tall trees on the island with strange creatures climbing among the branches. Glooskap shook his head sadly, for he had already learned in a dream that this was no island, but a three-masted sailing ship manned by pale-skinned strangers. Their arrival would bring many changes and he decided to take his leave. He set out in his birchbark canoe, the desolate cries of the seabirds mourning his departure. It is said that he lives on still, somewhere at the edge of the world, and will come again, when the time is right, to help and protect the world.

GLOSSARY

abundant Very plentiful; ample.

adobe Unburned, sundried brick, or the clay from which this brick is made.

ancestral Something inherited from someone earlier in the family line; something received from a forebear.

barren Not producing crops or fruit; having little or no vegetation.

barter To trade by exchanging goods and services without using money.

basin A wide, shallow, rounded hollow or depressed area in which the rock layers all incline toward a center.

burden Anything that is carried; a load.

conjure To summon something (like a spirit or devil) as if by a magic spell; to practice magic.

crest A plume or emblem placed atop an object, like a helmet, coat of arms, or totem pole.

decoy An artificial bird or animal used to lure game to a place where it can be killed or captured.

elaborate Worked out carefully; developed in great detail; highly wrought or ornamented; painstaking.

ermine A weasel whose brown fur turns white with a black-tipped tail in winter. The fur was often used for coats and robe trims.

exploit A bold, daring deed.

harpoon A barbed spear attached to a line used for catching whales and other large sea creatures.

heraldic Relating to genealogies, ancestry, and/or coats of arms.

iridescent Having or showing shifting changes of color or an interplay of rainbow-like colors.

mastodon Various large, extinct animals that resemble the elephant but were bigger.

mesa A small, high plateau or flat tableland with steep sides.

nomadic Having no permanent home and moving about constantly in search of food and pasture.

pendant An ornamental hanging object.

plateau An elevated tract of mostly level land.

prosperity Good fortune; wealth; success.

retaliation The act of returning an injury for an injury; payback.

sinew A tendon; a tough, inelastic, cord-like connective tissue that binds muscle to bone.

supernatural Not explainable by the known forces or laws of nature; attributable to God, a god, or spirits.

surplus A quantity of something over and above what is needed or used; excess; leftover.

travois A sled used by Native Americans of the North American Plains, composed of a net or platform atop two poles that served as the runners and were attached to a pulling horse or dog.

tropical The hot areas of the earth lying along the latitudes on either side of the equator.

weir A low dam or fence built in a river or stream, designed to back up or divert water and allow for the catching of fish.

American Indian Culture Research Center
P.O. Box 98
Marvin, SD 57251-0098
(605) 398-9200
Web site: http://www.bluecloud.org/
    dakota.html
The principal purpose of the center is to
    inform the general public of the world
    view, the philosophy of life, and the
    spiritual insight of native peoples.

American Indian Education Center (AIEC)
1314 Denison Road, Suite 102
Cleveland, OH 44109
(216) 351-4488
Web site: http://www.aiecc.net
The American Indian Education Center
    (AIEC) is an agency devoted to the
    cultural, educational, and socioeconomic
    enhancement of Native Americans through
    the provision of programs and services
    that empower all indigenous cultures
    with the holistic goal of developing self-
    sufficiency, self-determination, and self-
    esteem among all community members.

American Indian Policy Center
1463 Hewitt Avenue
St. Paul, MN 55104
(651) 644-1728
Web site: http://www.airpi.org
The center's mission is to provide
    government leaders, policy makers,
    and the public with accurate information
    about the legal and political history
    of Native American nations and the
    contemporary situation for Native
    Americans.

Assembly of First Nations (AFN)
Trebla Building
473 Albert Street, Suite 810
Ottawa, ON K1R 5B4
Canada
(613) 241-6789
Toll-Free: (866) 869-6789
Web site: http://www.afn.ca
The Assembly of First Nations (AFN) is the
    national organization representing First
    Nations citizens in Canada. The AFN
    represents all citizens regardless of age,
    gender, or place of residence.

National Congress of American
    Indians (NCAI)
1301 Connecticut Avenue NW, Suite 200
Washington, DC 20036
(202) 466-7767
Web site: http://www.ncai.org
The NCAI works to secure the rights and
    benefits to which Native Americans are
    entitled, to enlighten the public toward
    the better understanding of the Indian
    people, to preserve rights under Indian
    treaties or agreements with the United
    States, and to promote the common
    welfare of the Native Americans and
    Alaska Natives.

National Museum of the American
    Indian (NMAI)
4th Street and Independence Avenue SW
Washington, DC 20560
(202) 633-1000
Web site: http://www.nmai.si.edu
The National Museum of the American
    Indian (NMAI) has one of the most

extensive collections of Native American arts and artifacts in the world approximately 266,000 catalog records (825,000 items) representing more than 12,000 years of history and more than 1,200 indigenous cultures throughout the Americas.

Tribal Preservation Program
Heritage Preservation Services, National
    Park Service
1201 Eye Street NW 2255
Washington, DC 20005
(202) 354-1837
Web site: http://www.nps.gov/history/
    hps/tribal

The Tribal Preservation Program assists Native American tribes in preserving their historic properties and cultural traditions.

Web Sites

Due to the changing nature of Internet links, Rosen Publishing has developed an online list of Web sites related to the subject of this book. This site is updated regularly. Please use this link to access this list:

http://www.rosenlinks.com/anc/amer

FOR FURTHER READING

Bruchac, Joseph. *Our Stories Remember: American Indian History, Culture, and Values Through Storytelling.* Golden, CO: Fulcrum Publishing, 2003.

Chatlien, Ruth Hull. *Modern American Indian Chiefs.* Broomall, PA: Mason Crest Publishers, 2009.

Johnson, Troy R. *Red Power: The Native American Civil Rights Movement.* New York, NY: Chelsea House Publications, 2007.

Kavin, Kim. *Tools of Native Americans: A Kid's Guide to the History and Culture of the First Americans.* White River Junction, VT: Nomad Press, 2006.

Larned, W. T. *American Indian Fairy Tales.* Whitefish, MT: Kessinger Publishing, LLC, 2007.

McMaster, Gerald, and Clifford E. Trafzer, eds. *Native Universe: Voices of Indian Americans.* Des Moines, IA: National Geographic, 2008.

Murdoch, David S. *North American Indian (DK Eyewitness Books).* New York, NY: DK Children, 2005.

Pritzker, Barry M. *A Native American Encyclopedia.* New York, NY: Oxford University Press, 2000.

Waldman, Carl. *Atlas of the North American Indian.* New York, NY: Checkmark Books, 2000.

Waldman, Carl. *Encyclopedia of Native American Tribes.* New York, NY: Facts on File, 2006.

INDEX

48